CW00728248

If so, you may be in a vicious cycle

When you feel low or stressed, you may cut down or stop doing various things you used to enjoy. Maybe you don't go out so much, you avoid seeing friends and you may even stop listening to music or watching sport?

Instead we focus on doing things we think we "*must/ought/got to*" do. Things like going to work, looking after children, or older parents - things like these.

It feels like such a relief when we cut down on other activities to help us get through each day. But if you do this, you can end up feeling even worse.

Turn over to see the vicious cycle in action

THE LESS YOU DO, THE WORSE YOU FEEL, THE WORSE YOU FEEL, THE LESS YOU DO

living
life to
the full
www.llttf.com

The vicious cycle of reduced activity

Download from
www.llttf.com

You feel worse:
Low/feeling down
Poor sleep and energy
Feeling physically unwell

1

Everything seems harder:
Things seem pointless and too much effort
Not enjoying things
Going through the motions

2

Life gets smaller and smaller

4

Count the cost:
Your world gets smaller
You feel even worse
Lose confidence
... and the Cycle spins

3

Cut down/avoid things:
Only do things you think you must/should/ought to do
It's a relief to cut down/stop activities even when they are good for us

Turn over to break the cycle

Copyright Five Areas Resources Ltd (2023). Used under licence.
Download more for free from www.llttf.com

DO YOU KNOW WHAT YOU JUST DID?

VERY GOOD

You broke the cycle of reduced activity!

All it took was a decision - turning that page.

Now all you have to do is take another tiny step, then another and another.

What steps? That's what this book is about – to show you the easy steps you can take to break that cycle and start feeling better. It involves making choices. Choosing to do things that help you feel better, rather than choosing to hide away doing less and less.

Important point coming up

IT HELPS TO HAVE A DAILY ROUTINE THAT FITS WITH YOUR WORK AND LIFE COMMITMENTS - AND GIVES YOU A STRUCTURE TO YOUR DAY

When things seem hard, it's easy to lose your daily routine. It's tempting to lie in bed longer, stay up later, or have a longer nap each afternoon. But before you know it **you can lose the pattern and structure of your day and week.**

What time do you typically get up?

… and go to bed?

These are the anchors that start and end your day. Have they changed from your usual pattern? Other anchors that split your day are mealtimes. So, when do you eat?

Breakfast?

Lunch?

Your evening meal?

Together, these anchors define your morning, afternoon, and evening - as well as your time in bed. Around these points are all the other activities of the day. Meeting friends, work, household chores, going for a walk and more. **It helps to get a routine going again that balances activities across the day and week.** Then start adding things in that you know are good for you over the next few weeks.

First, look at what you do just now

THINK ABOUT YESTERDAY

Start by thinking about the last 24 hours. Write down a list of things you have done. Include things like getting dressed, watching TV, talking to a friend, showering, washing your hair, etc. Then tick the activity for whether it gave you a sense of pleasure, achievement or feeling close/connected to other people. The first two spaces are filled in to show you how to do it.

	Pleasure	Achievement	Closeness
Talking to my friend	✓	☐	✓
Cleaning a room	☐	✓	☐
	☐	☐	☐
	☐	☐	☐
	☐	☐	☐
	☐	☐	☐
	☐	☐	☐
	☐	☐	☐
	☐	☐	☐
	☐	☐	☐
	☐	☐	☐

Have a look at your list. Has it changed over time? If so, what is different?

ANYTHING MISSING FROM YOUR DAY?

What activities did you used to enjoy but haven't felt like doing lately?

Fun/pleasure

- [ ] Enjoying sport (watching or taking part)
- [ ] Listening to music/going to a concert/show
- [ ] Watching a film/going to the cinema
- [ ] Doing a hobby
- [ ] Watching TV
- [ ] Going for a walk/getting some fresh air
- [ ] Doing exercise/swimming/running/gym
- [ ] Reading a good book, magazine or listening to a podcast
- [ ] Practicing relaxation techniques/yoga/pilates etc.

What about things you've stopped doing?

Download from
www.llttf.com

Getting things done/achievement:

☐ Learning something new/attending a class

☐ Learning a new skill like a musical instrument, a language, or to drive

☐ Planning and cooking regular meals

☐ Making your house look good (ironing, cleaning, tidying)

Spending time with people you like/ Closeness:

☐ Seeing your friends, relatives or other people you like

☐ Phoning or texting friends/keeping in touch with others

☐ Going to church, mosque, temple or synagogue if that's important to you

☐ Going to a match and supporting your team with others

Routine:

☐ Spending time with your pets (e.g. walking the dog)

☐ Keeping to regular mealtimes/bed time/time to get up

☐ Keeping up with the garden/looking after house plants that add colour to your life

Now choose an activity you want to build

Copyright Five Areas Resources Ltd (2023). Used under licence.
Download more for free from www.llttf.com

13

USE WHAT YOU'VE FOUND TO START RE-BALANCING YOUR DAY

To feel better again, pick some activities from your list and build them up in your life.

One of the reasons we feel worse when we cut down or stop doing things, is the fact that it's usually the things we like that we cut down on first.

To start it picking up, you need to choose good things to fill your day with. Not all the time – just plan one thing at first. Remember, the things that make you smile? Pick one thing that used to give you pleasure, or a sense of achievement. Or something that you think is worthwhile or made you feel close to others.

Just one thing to start with. Something that you think you can do - not too big a challenge so it seems too hard. Or too small so it will hardly make a difference.

NOW WRITE
IT HERE
SO YOU DON'T
FORGET IT

_____

_____

GOOD!

You've just written down the thing you're going to start doing again. Something worth getting up for.

Now, you're going to do it

NOW CHOOSE WHEN YOU'LL DO IT

Today

09.00

09.30

10.00

10.30 **Do my thing now.**

11.00

Say *what* and *when*

Think about the activity you want to do first.

Look at your phone or printed diary or calendar. Pick a time that's currently free. Then, go, ahead, write it in.

You don't want it to feel lonely, so soon you'll be adding other activities into your calendar.

But to start with, just include the single activity you planned - the one you wrote down on page 15.

The aim over time is to plan a mix of activities across your day and week.

Now let's add in some more activities

REBUILD YOUR ROUTINE

Get into a basic daily routine - a time to get up, eat and go to bed. Slowly add in the things you want to build up in your life. Things like doing the household chores. Or perhaps going for a walk, meeting friends or attending a regular class?

Having to get out of bed to walk the dog or feed the baby can be a real pain, especially on cold mornings, but it's also a great way to feel better. No dog? No baby? You can still go for a walk on your own. Getting up and showering. Eating breakfast. Playing your music. Getting on the bus. Cleaning the house. Can't get out? Make the most of the activities you can do.

And if you rebuild your routine with things that involve others (ringing a relative each morning, walking with a friend every Wednesday) you'll feel even better because of that feeling of closeness we mentioned before.

It needs to be a daily routine, too. Choose something every single day that you need to get up and out of bed for. **Don't lie in** - remember, the less you do the worse you feel, the worse you feel, the less you do.

More good stuff on the next page

ADD SOME MORE ACTIVITIES THAT ARE GOOD FOR YOU

Plan a series of other activities, then add them one by one into your Calendar. Make each activity small and not too difficult. Don't be too ambitious, be easy on yourself.

- Choose from the activities you've identified on your ticklist on pages 12-13 that help you feel better.
- Add in some of the things you've cut down or stopped doing.
- Choose things you value and give a sense of pleasure, achievement or closeness.
- Build things up over a few weeks so you end up with one activity planned each day.
- Leave some gaps for the unexpected things that crop up. Also allow some times just for you.

With each activity you add, you're breaking that vicious cycle, and making it spin the other way so you feel better and better.

Are you ignoring important things?

Some activities may seem hard or boring. Perhaps, things like paying the bills, looking after yourself, keeping up with the housework. They can all seem too much trouble when you're feeling low or stressed.

The problem is some activities are **necessary,** and if you don't do them it makes you feel worse. So here's what to do: choose one important task that wasn't in your diary but should have been, and plan to do it.

Pay that bill. Make that call. Get your hair done. Do some tidying. Wash the dishes. Plan what you will do, and when you'll do it.

You'll feel a lot better afterwards and you'll be able to add it to your diary and put a tick in the 'achievement' box!

Summary: Aim for the following

Across each day and week you need to get a mix of activities that help you feel better.

Start with the things you can change most easily. Aim for variety so you address each of the key areas:

1. **Pleasure:** things that make you feel good.

2. **Achievement:** things you value and are important to tick off your list as "done".

3. **Closeness:** where you connect with people you like or are important to you.

4. Finally don't forget to do **the key essentials** that you need to complete or it will cause you problems.

Each of these activities breaks the vicious cycle and makes you feel better. But don't rush. Some activities need to be built up to slowly.

TAKING SMALL STEPS THAT MOVE YOU FORWARDS

Some activities may be good for you, but seem just too hard to do all at once.

You need to work up to doing them step by step.

For example, if you have lots of chores to do around the house ...

Choose one room and one task first.

Or set yourself a fixed time to work at something. For example, allocate half an hour for the ironing. If you struggle to do that, choose a target that works for you such as doing three items of ironing rather than setting yourself a larger goal that is too much for you at this time.

It's important with goals to choose activities based on how you are now - not on what you used to do before.

SOUNDS EASY DOESN'T IT?

But you know change sometimes isn't that easy

Remember all those failed New Year's resolutions? Promises to change that seem hard? Or maybe we forget, or find we can't be bothered, or talk ourselves out of things?

So, let's recognise something. It's often hard to make changes. That's why we've asked you to pick activities to do that you know can be good for you.

But if you find you get stuck doing a particular activity, here's a helping hand to make a plan to do it that will work.

Turn over to complete a Planner Sheet

Planner Sheet

Make a Plan!

1. What am I going to do?

Just one small thing

2. When am I going to do it?

That way you'll know if you don't do it

3. What problems or difficulties could arise, and how can I overcome them?